CONSTITUTION OF THE ITALIAN REPUBLIC

This edition published by Lector House in 2024

ISBN: 978-93-5800-981-1

Lector House LLP
Registered Office: H. No. 96, Block C, Tomar Colony,
Burari, Delhi – 110084, India
info@lectorhouse.com
www.lectorhouse.com

CONSTITUTION OF THE ITALIAN REPUBLIC

SENATE OF THE REPUBLIC

2024

LECTOR HOUSE LLP

CONSTITUTION OF THE ITALIAN REPUBLIC

SENATE OF THE REPUBLIC

CONTENTS

CONSTITUTION OF THE ITALIAN REPUBLIC

THE PROVISIONAL HEAD OF STATE

whereas the Constituent Assembly approved the Constitution of the Republic of Italy on 22 December 1947;

By virtue of Final Provision XVIII of the Constitution;

ENACTS

The Constitution of the Republic of Italy in the following text:

FUNDAMENTAL PRINCIPLES

Article 1

Italy is a democratic Republic founded on labour.

Sovereignty shall belong to the people and be exercised by the people in the forms and within the limits of this Constitution.

Article 2

The Republic shall recognise and protect the inviolable rights of the person, both as an individual and in the social groups where human personality is expressed. The Republic expects that the fundamental duties of political, economic and social solidarity be fulfilled.

Article 3

All citizens shall have equal social dignity and shall be equal before the law, without distinction of gender, race, language, religion, political opinion, personal and social conditions.

It shall be the duty of the Republic to remove those obstacles of an economic or social nature which constrain the freedom and equality of citizens, thereby impeding the full development of the human person and the effective participation of all workers in the political, economic and social organisation of the country.

Article 4

The Republic shall recognise the right of all citizens to work and shall promote such conditions as shall render this right effective.

Every citizen shall have the duty, according to personal potential and individual choice, to perform any activity or function contributing to the material or spiritual progress of society.

Article 5

The Republic shall be one and indivisible. It shall recognise and promote local autonomies and implement the fullest measure of administrative decentralisation of those services which are provided by the State. The Republic shall adapt the principles and methods of its legislation to the requirements of autonomy and decentralisation.

Article 6

The Republic shall safeguard language minorities by means of appropriate measures.

Article 7

The State and the Catholic Church shall be independent and sovereign, each within its own sphere.

Their relations shall be regulated by the Lateran pacts. Amendments to such Pacts which are accepted by both parties shall not require the procedure of constitutional amendments.

Article 8

All religious denominations shall be equally free before the law.

Denominations other than Catholicism shall have the right to self-organisation according to their own statutes, provided these do not conflict with Italian law.

Their relations with the State shall be regulated by law, based on agreements with their respective representatives.

Article 9

The Republic shall promote the development of culture and scientific and technical research.

It shall safeguard natural landscape and the historical and artistic heritage of the Nation.

Article 10

The Italian legal system shall conform to the generally recognised principles of international law. The legal status of foreigners shall be regulated by law in compliance with international provisions and treaties.

A foreign national, who is denied – in his or her country – the enjoyment of the democratic freedoms established by this Constitution shall be entitled to the right of asylum in the Republic under such conditions as shall be established by law.

A foreign national may not be extradited for a political offence.

Article 11

Italy rejects war as an instrument of aggression against the freedom of other peoples and as a means for the settlement of international disputes. Italy shall agree, on conditions of equality with other States, to such limitations of sovereignty as may be necessary to ensure peace and justice among Nations. Italy shall promote and encourage international organisations pursuing such goals.

Article 12

The flag of the Republic shall be the Italian tricolour of three green, white and red vertical bands of equal size.

PART I

RIGHTS AND DUTIES OF CITIZENS

TITLE I

CIVIL RELATIONS

Article 13

Personal liberty shall be inviolable.

No one may be detained, inspected, or searched nor otherwise subjected to any restriction of personal liberty except by reasoned order of the Judiciary and only in such cases and in such manner as provided by the law.

In exceptional circumstances and under such conditions of necessity and urgency as shall conclusively be defined by the law, the police may take provisional measures that shall be referred within 48 hours to the Judiciary for validation and which, in default of such validation in the following 48 hours, shall be revoked and considered null and void.

Any act of physical and moral violence against a person subjected to restriction of personal liberty shall be punished.

The law shall establish the maximum duration of preventive detention.

Article 14

Personal domicile shall be inviolable.

Home inspections, searches, or seizures shall not be admissible save in such cases and manners as shall be established by the law and in compliance with provisions safeguarding personal liberty.

Controls and inspections for reason of public health and safety, or for economic and fiscal purposes, shall be regulated by appropriate laws.

Article 15

Freedom and confidentiality of correspondence and of every other form of communication shall be inviolable.

Limitations may only be imposed by reasoned judicial decision and in accordance with the safeguards provided by the law.

Article 16

Every citizen has the right to reside and travel freely in any part of the country, except for such general limitations as may be established by law for reasons of health or security. No restrictions may be imposed for political reasons.

Every citizen shall be free to leave the territory of the Republic and return to it, notwithstanding any legal obligations.

Article 17

Citizens may assemble peaceably and unarmed. No previous notice is required for meetings, including those held in places open the public.

In case of meetings held in public places, prior notice shall be given to the authorities, who may prohibit such meetings only for proven reason of security or public safety.

Article 18

Citizens may form associations freely and without authorization for any ends that are not forbidden by criminal law.

Secret associations and associations that, even indirectly, pursue political aims through organisations of a military nature shall be forbidden.

Article 19

Everyone shall be entitled to profess freely their religious beliefs in any form, individually or with others, and to promote such beliefs and celebrate rites in public or in private, provided they are not offensive to public morality.

Article 20

No special limitation or tax burden shall be imposed on the establishment, legal capacity or activities of any organisation on the ground of its religious nature or its religious or confessional goals.

Article 21

Everyone has the right to freely express their thoughts in speech, writing, or any other form of communication.

The press may not be subjected to any authorisations or censorship.

Seizure may be permitted only by reasoned judicial order and only for offences expressly determined by the law on the press or in case of violation of the obligation to identify the persons responsible for such offences.

In such cases, when there is absolute urgency and timely intervention of the Judiciary is not possible, a periodical may be confiscated by the criminal police, which shall immediately and in no case later than 24 hours refer the matter to the Judiciary for validation. In default of such validation in the following 24 hours, the measure shall be revoked and considered null and void.

The law may introduce general provisions for the disclosure of financial sources of periodical publications.

Publications, performances, and other exhibits offensive to public morality shall be prohibited. Prevention and enforcement relating to such violations shall be established by law.

Article 22

No-one may be deprived of their legal capacity, citizenship, or name for political reasons.

Article 23

No obligation of a personal or financial nature may be imposed on anyone except by law.

Article 24

Anyone may bring cases before a court of law in order to protect their rights under civil and administrative law.

Defence is an inviolable right at every stage and instance of legal proceedings.

The poor are entitled by law to proper means for action or defence in all courts.

The law shall determine the conditions and forms regulating damages in case of judicial errors.

Article 25

No case may be removed from the court seized with it as established by law.

No punishment may be inflicted except by virtue of a law in force at the time the offence was committed.

No restriction may be placed on a person's liberty save for as provided by law.

Article 26

Extradition of a citizen may be granted only if it is expressly envisaged by international conventions.

In any case, extradition may not be permitted for political offences.

Article 27

Criminal responsibility is personal.

A defendant shall be considered not guilty until a final sentence has been passed.

Punishments may not be inhuman and shall aim at re-educating the convicted.

Death penalty is prohibited.

Article 28

Officials of the State or public agencies shall be directly responsible under criminal, civil, and administrative law for acts committed in violation of rights. In such cases, civil liability shall extend to the State and to such public agencies.

TITLE II

ETHICAL AND SOCIAL RELATIONS

Article 29

The Republic shall recognise the rights of the family as a natural society founded on marriage.

Marriage shall be based on the moral and legal equality of the spouses within the limits laid down by law to ensure family unity.

Article 30

It is the duty and right of parents to support, raise and educate their children, even if born out of wedlock.

Is case of incapacity of the parents, the law shall provide for the fulfilment of their duties.

The law shall ensure any children born out of wedlock the same legal and social protection measures as are recognised to the members of the legitimate family.

The law shall establish rules and limits for the determination of paternity.

Article 31

The Republic shall assist the development of a family and the fulfilment of its duties, with particular consideration for large families, through economic measures and other benefits.

The Republic shall protect mothers, children and the young by adopting necessary provisions.

Article 32

The Republic shall safeguard health as a fundamental right of the individual and as a collective interest, and shall ensure free medical care to the indigent.

No-one may be obliged to undergo any health treatment except under the provisions of the law. The law may not under any circumstances violate the limits imposed by respect for the human person.

Article 33

Arts and science shall be free and may be freely taught.

The Republic shall lay down general rules for education and shall establish State schools of all types and levels.

Entities and private persons shall have the right to establish schools and institutions of education, at no cost for the State.

The law, when setting out the rights and obligations for non-State schools applying for recognition, shall ensure that such schools enjoy full liberty and offer their pupils an education and qualifications of the same standards as those afforded to pupils in State schools.

A State examination shall be required for admission to and graduation from the various types and levels of schools and to acquire qualification to exercise a profession.

Higher education institutions, universities and academies, shall have the right to establish their own regulations within the limits established by the law.

Article 34

Education shall be open to everyone.

Primary education, given for at least eight years, shall be compulsory and free.

Capable and deserving pupils, including those lacking financial resources, shall have the right to attain the highest levels of education.

The Republic shall render this right effective through scholarships, allowances to families and other benefits, which shall be assigned through competitive examinations.

TITLE III
ECONOMIC RELATIONS

Article 35

The Republic shall protect labour in all its forms and practices.

It shall provide for the training and professional advancement of workers.

It shall promote and encourage international agreements and organisations which have the aim of establishing and regulating labour rights.

It shall recognise the freedom to emigrate, subject to general-interest obligations established by law, and shall protect Italian workers abroad.

Article 36

Workers shall be entitled to a remuneration commensurate to the quantity and quality of their work and in any case such as to ensure them and their families a free and dignified existence.

The maximum daily working hours shall be established by law.

Workers shall have the right to a weekly rest day and paid yearly holidays. They may not waive this right.

Article 37

Women workers shall be entitled to equal rights and equal pay as men for similar jobs. Working conditions shall allow women to fulfil their essential role in the family and ensure appropriate protection for the mother and child.

The law shall establish the minimum age for paid labour.

The Republic shall protect the work of children by means of special provisions and shall ensure that children enjoy equal pay for equal work.

Article 38

Every citizen unable to work and without the necessary means of subsistence shall be entitled to welfare support.

Workers shall be entitled to adequate means for their living requirements in case of accidents, illness, disability, old age and involuntary unemployment.

Physically and mentally disabled persons shall be entitled to education and vocational training.

Responsibilities under this Article shall be entrusted to entities and institutions established or supported by the State.

Private-sector assistance may be freely provided.

Article 39

Trade unions may be freely established.

No obligations may be imposed on trade unions other than registration at local or central offices, according to the provisions of the law.

A prerequisite for registration is that the statutes of trade unions establish their internal organisation on a democratic basis.

Registered trade unions shall be considered legal persons. Through unified representations proportional to their memberships, they may enter into collective labour agreements that have a mandatory effect for all persons belonging to the categories under the agreement.

Article 40

The right to strike shall be exercised in compliance with the law.

Article 41

Private economic enterprise shall be free.

It may not be carried out against the common good or in such a manner that could damage safety, liberty and human dignity.

The law shall provide for appropriate programmes and controls so that public and private-sector economic activity may be oriented and co-ordinated for social purposes.

Article 42

Property shall be public or private. Economic assets may belong to the State, to public bodies or to private persons.

Private property shall be recognised and protected by the law, which shall determine how it can be acquired, enjoyed and restrained so as to ensure its social function and render it accessible to all.

In the cases provided for by the law and with provisions for compensation, private property may be expropriated for reasons of general interest.

The law shall regulate and limit legitimate and testamentary inheritance and the rights of the State in matters of inheritance.

Article 43

For the purposes of the common good, the law may establish that an enterprise or a category there-of be, through compulsory purchase authority and subject to compensation, reserved to the Government, a public agency, a workers' or users' association, provided that such enterprise operates in the field of essential public services, energy sources or monopolies and is of general public interest.

Article 44

For the purpose of ensuring a rational use of land and equitable social relationships, the law shall impose obligations and constraints on private land ownership; set limitations to the size of property according to the region and the agricultural area; encourage and impose land reclamation, the conversion of large estates and the reorganisation of farm units; and assist small and medium-sized properties.

The law shall make provisions for mountain areas.

Article 45

The Republic shall recognises the social function of co-operation of a mutually supportive, non-speculative nature. The law shall promote and encourage cooperation through appropriate means and ensure its character and purposes through appropriate control mechanisms.

The law shall safeguard and promote the handicrafts.

Article 46

For the purposes of economic and social betterment of workers and consistently with the requirements of production, the Republic shall recognise the rights of workers to collaborate in the management of enterprises, in the forms and within the limits established by law.

Article 47

The Republic shall encourage and protect savings in all forms. It shall regulate, co-ordinate and oversee credit activities.

The Republic shall promote house and farm ownership and direct and indirect shareholding in major national enterprises through the use of private savings.

TITLE IV
POLITICAL RELATIONS

Article 48

Any citizen, male or female, who has attained the age of majority, shall be a voter.

The vote is personal and equal, free and secret.

The exercise thereof is a civic duty.

The law shall lay down the requirements and modalities for citizens residing abroad to exercise their right to vote and shall ensure that this right be effective. A constituency of Italians abroad shall be established for elections to Parliament; the number of seats for such constituency shall be established under this Constitution and under the law.

The right to vote may not be restricted except for civil incapacity, or following an irrevocable conviction or in case of moral unworthiness as shall be laid down by law.

Article 49

Any citizen shall have the right to freely establish political parties in order to contribute to the development of national policies through the democratic process.

Article 50

Any citizen may submit petitions to Parliament to request legislative measures or to express collective needs.

Article 51

Any citizen of either sex is eligible for public and elected offices on equal terms, according to the requirements established by law. To this end, the Republic shall adopt specific measures to promote equal opportunities between women and men.

The law may grant Italians who are not resident in the Republic the same rights as citizens for the purposes of access to public and elected offices.

Whoever is elected to a public function shall be entitled to the time needed to perform that function and to retain a previously held job.

Article 52

Defence of the motherland is a sacred duty for every citizen.

Military service is obligatory within the limits and in the manner set by law. Its fulfilment shall not prejudice a citizen's job, nor the exercise of their political rights.

The organisation of the armed forces shall be based on the democratic spirit of the Republic.

Article 53

Every person shall contribute to public expenditure in accordance with their capabilities.

The tax system shall be progressive.

Article 54

All citizens have the duty to be loyal to the Republic and to uphold its Constitution and laws.

Those citizens to whom public functions are entrusted shall have the duty to fulfil such functions with discipline and honour, taking an oath in those cases established by law.

PART II
ORGANISATION OF THE REPUBLIC

TITLE I

PARLIAMENT

SECTION I. – *The Houses of Parliament*

Article 55

Parliament shall consist of the Chamber of deputies and the Senate of the Republic.

Parliament shall meet in joint session only in cases established by this Constitution.

Article 56

The Chamber of deputies shall be elected by universal direct suffrage.

The number of deputies is six hundred and thirty, twelve of which are elected in the overseas constituency.

All voters who have attained the age of twenty-five on the day of elections shall be eligible to be deputies.

The division of seats among the constituencies, with the exception of the seats of the overseas constituency, shall be calculated by dividing the number of inhabitants of the Republic, as per the latest general census, by six hundred and eighteen and by distributing the seats in proportion to the population in every constituency, on the basis of whole shares and highest remainders.

Article 57

The Senate of the Republic shall be elected on a regional basis, with the exception of the seats of the overseas constituency.

The number of senators to be elected is three hundred and fifteen, six of whom are elected in the overseas constituency.

No Region may have fewer than seven Senators; Molise shall have two, Valle d'Aosta one.

The division of seats among Regions, with the exception of the number of seats assigned to the overseas constituency and in accordance with the provisions of Article 56 above, shall be calculated in proportion to the population of each Region as per the latest general census, on the basis of whole shares and highest remainders.

Article 58

Senators shall be elected by universal direct suffrage by voters who are over twenty-five years of age.

Voters who have attained the age of forty shall be eligible to the Senate.

Article 59

Former Presidents of the Republic shall be ex officio life Senators unless they renounce the office.

The President of the Republic may appoint as life Senators five citizens who have honoured the Nation through their outstanding achievements in the social, scientific, artistic and literary fields.

Article 60

The Chamber of deputies and the Senate of the Republic shall be elected for five years.

The term for each House may not be extended, save by law and only in the case of war.

Article 61

Elections for a new Parliament shall take place within seventy days from the end of the term of the previous Parliament. A new Parliament shall be convened no later than twenty days following the election.

Until such time as the new Parliament meets, the authority of the previous Parliament shall be extended.

Article 62

In default of any other arrangements, Parliament shall be convened on the first working day of February and October.

Each House may be convened in special session on the initiative of its President, the President of the Republic or a third of its members.

When one House is convened in special session, the other House shall be convened as a matter of course.

Article 63

Each House shall elect a President and a Bureau from among its members.

When Parliament meets in joint session, the President and the Bureau shall be those of the Chamber of deputies.

Article 64

Each House shall adopt its own Rules by an absolute majority of its members.

Sittings shall be public; however, either House and Parliament in joint session may decide to convene an in camera sitting.

A decision of a House and of Parliament shall not be valid unless a majority of members is present, and such decision is passed by a majority of members present, save for those cases where a special majority is required under the Constitution.

Members of the Government, even if they are not members of Parliament, shall have the right and, if so requested, the obligation to attend the sittings. They shall be heard every time they so request.

Article 65

The law shall determine the cases of disqualification from the office of deputy or senator.

No one may be a member of both Houses at the same time.

Article 66

Each House shall verify the credentials of its members and the causes of disqualification that may arise at a later stage.

Article 67

Each Member of Parliament shall represent the Nation and carry out their duties without a binding mandate.

Article 68

Members of Parliament may not be held liable for the opinions expressed or votes cast in the performance of their function.

In default of the authorisation of his or her House, no Member of Parliament may be subjected to personal or home search, nor may he or she be arrested or otherwise deprived of personal freedom, nor held in custody, except when a final court sentence is enforced, or when a Member is apprehended in the act of committing an offence for which arrest flagrante delicto is mandatory.

Such an authorization shall also be required in order to intercept a Member's conversations or communications, or to forfeit a Member's mail.

Article 69

Members of Parliament shall receive an allowance established by law.

Section II. – *The Making of Legislation*

Article 70

The law-making function shall be exercised collectively by both Houses.

Article 71

Legislation may be introduced by the Government, by a Member of Parliament or by such agencies and bodies as may be so empowered by constitutional amendment law.

The people may initiate legislation by proposing a bill drawn up in sections and signed by at least fifty thousand voters.

Article 72

A bill introduced in either House of Parliament shall, under the Rules of procedure of such House, be referred to a Committee and then to the plenary, which shall consider it section by section and then put it to the final vote.

The Rules shall establish shorter procedures to consider a bill that has been declared urgent.

The Rules may also establish when and how a bill may be considered and definitively passed by a Committee, including a Standing Committee, composed so as to reflect the proportion of Parliamentary Groups. Even in such cases, a bill under committee scrutiny may be referred back to the plenary, if the Government or one-tenth of the members of the House or one-fifth of the Committee request that it be debated and voted on by the House or that it be submitted to the House for final approval, following explanations of vote. The Rules shall establish how committee proceedings are made public.

The ordinary procedure for consideration and direct approval in plenary shall always be followed for bills on constitutional and electoral matters, delegation of law-making authority, ratification of international treaties, approval of budgets and accounts.

Article 73

Laws shall be promulgated by the President of the Republic within one month of their approval. If a House of Parliament, following a decision adopted by an absolute majority of its members, declares a law to be urgent, such law shall be promulgated within the deadline established therein.

A law shall be published immediately after promulgation and come into force on the fifteenth day following publication, unless such law establishes a different deadline.

Article 74

The President of the Republic may send Parliament a reasoned opinion to request that a law scheduled for promulgation be considered anew.

If such law is passed again, it shall be promulgated.

Article 75

A general referendum may be held to repeal, in whole or in part, a law or a measure having he force of law, when so requested by five hundred thousand voters or five Regional Councils.

No referendum may be held on a law regulating taxes, the budget, amnesty or pardon, or a law ratifying an international treaty.

Any citizen entitled to vote for the Chamber of deputies shall have the right to vote in a referendum.

The referendum shall be considered to have been carried if the majority of those eligible has voted and a majority of valid votes has been achieved.

The law shall establish the procedures to hold a referendum.

Article 76

The law-making function may not be delegated to the Government unless principles and criteria have been established and then only for a limited time and for specific purposes.

Article 77

The Government may not, without a delegation from Parliament, issue a decree having force of law. When the Government, in case of necessity and urgency, adopts under its own responsibility a temporary measure, it shall submit such measure to Parliament for enactment. During dissolution, Parliament shall be convened within five days after any such measure has been submitted.

Such a measure shall lose effect from the beginning unless it is transposed into law by Parliament within sixty days of its publication. Parliament may regulate the legal relations arisen from a rejected decree.

Article 78

Parliament has the authority to declare a state of war and vest the necessary powers into the Government.

Article 79

Amnesty and pardon may be granted by a law adopted by a two-thirds majority in both Houses of Parliament, on each Article and on the final vote.

Such law shall set the deadline for the implementation of amnesty or pardon.

Amnesty and pardon thus introduced may not be granted in case of a crime committed after the introduction of such bill.

Article 80

Parliament shall authorise by law the ratification of such international treaties as have a political nature, require arbitration or legal settlements, entail border changes, new expenditure or new legislation.

Article 81

The State shall balance revenue and expenditure in its budget, taking account of any adverse and favourable phases of economic cycles.

No recourse shall be made to borrowing except for the purposes of taking account of the effects of an economic cycle or, subject to authorisation by Parliament passed by an absolute majority vote of members, in exceptional circumstances.

Any law involving new or increased expenditure shall provide for the resources to cover such expenditure.

Every year Parliament shall pass a law approving the budget and the accounts submitted by the Government.

Provisional budget implementation shall not be allowed except by an Act of Parliament and only for a period not exceeding four months in total.

The content of the budget law, the fundamental rules and the criteria adopted to ensure balance between revenue and expenditure and the sustainability of general government debt shall be established by an Act of Parliament approved by an absolute majority of the Members of each House in compliance with the principles established by a constitutional amendment act.

Article 82

Each House of Parliament may conduct enquiries on matters of public interest.

For this purpose, it shall detail from among its members a Committee formed in such a way so as to represent the proportionality of existing Parliamentary Groups. A Committee of Enquiry may conduct investigations and examination with the same powers and limitations as the judiciary.

TITLE II

THE PRESIDENT OF THE REPUBLIC

Article 83

The President of the Republic shall be elected by Parliament in joint session.

Three delegates from each Region, as shall have been elected by their respective Regional Councils so as to ensure the representation of the opposition, shall participate in the election. Valle d'Aosta shall have one delegate.

The President of the Republic shall be elected by secret ballot by a majority of two thirds of the assembly. After the third ballot an absolute majority shall suffice.

Article 84

Any citizen who has attained fifty years of age and enjoys civil and political rights may be elected President of the Republic.

The office of President of the Republic shall be incompatible with any other office.

The remuneration and entitlements of the President shall be established by law.

Article 85

The President of the Republic shall be elected for seven years.

Thirty days before the expiration of the term, the President of the Chamber of Deputies shall summon a joint session of Parliament and regional delegates to elect a new President of the Republic.

During dissolution of Parliament or in the three-month period prior to dissolution, the election shall be held within the first fifteen days of the first sitting of a new Parliament. In the intervening time, the powers of the incumbent President shall be extended.

Article 86

The functions of the President of the Republic, in all cases in which the President cannot discharge them, shall be performed by the President of the Senate.

In case of permanent incapacity or death or resignation of the President of the Republic, the President of the Chamber of Deputies shall call the election of a new President of the Republic within fifteen days, notwithstanding the longer term envisaged during dissolution of Parliament or in the three months preceding dissolution.

Article 87

The President of the Republic is the Head of the State and represents national unity.

The President may send messages to Parliament.

The President shall call the election of a new Parliament and set the date of its first sitting.

The President shall authorise the introduction to Parliament of bills submitted by the Government.

The President shall enact laws, and issue decrees having force of law and regulations.

The President shall call a general referendum in the cases provided for by the Constitution.

The President shall appoint State officials in the cases provided for by the law.

The President shall accredit and receive diplomats and ratify international treaties that have, where required, been authorised by Parliament.

The President shall be the commander-in-chief of the armed forces, shall preside over the Supreme Council of Defence established by law, and shall make declarations of war as have been agreed by Parliament.

The President shall preside over the High Council for the Judiciary.

The President may grant pardons and commute punishments.

The President shall confer the honorary distinctions of the Republic.

Article 88

In consultation with the presiding officers of Parliament, the President may dissolve one or both Houses of Parliament.

The President of the Republic may not exercise such right during the final six months of the presidential term, unless said period coincides in full or in part with the final six months of Parliament.

Article 89

A writ of the President of the Republic shall not be valid unless signed by the proposing Minister, who shall be accountable for it.

A writ having force of law and other writs issued by virtue of a law shall be countersigned by the President of the Council of Ministers.

Article 90

The President of the Republic shall not be responsible for the actions performed in the exercise of presidential duties, except in case of high treason or attack on the Constitution.

In such cases, the President may be impeached by Parliament in joint session, with an absolute majority of its members.

Article 91

Before taking office, the President of the Republic shall take an oath of allegiance to the Republic and pledge to uphold the Constitution before Parliament in joint session.

TITLE III

GOVERNMENT

Section I. – *The Council of Ministers*

Article 92

The Government of the Republic is made up of the President of the Council and the Ministers who together form the Council of Ministers.

The President of the Republic shall appoint a President of the Council of Ministers, on whose proposal the President of the Republic shall appoint Ministers.

Article 93

Before taking office, the President of the Council of Ministers and the Ministers shall be sworn in by the President of the Republic.

Article 94

The Government must receive the confidence of both Houses of Parliament.

Each House shall grant or withdraw its confidence through a reasoned motion voted by roll-call. Within ten days of its establishment the Government shall come before Parliament to obtain confidence.

Rejection of a Government proposal by one or both Houses, shall not call for resignation of the Government.

A motion of no-confidence must be signed by at least one-tenth of the members of a House and may be debated at least three days following its submission.

Article 95

The President of the Council shall conduct and be accountable for the general policy of the Government. The President of the Council shall ensure the consistency of political and administrative policies, by promoting and co-ordinating the activities of Ministers.

The Ministers shall be collectively responsible for the decisions of the Council of Ministers; they shall be individually responsible for the decisions of their own ministries.

The law shall establish the organisation of the Presidency of the Council, as well as the number, competence and organisation of ministries.

Article 96

The President of the Council of Ministers and the Ministers, even if no more in office, shall be subject to ordinary justice for any crimes committed in the exercise of their duties, provided authorisation is given by the Senate of the Republic or the Chamber of Deputies, in accordance with the norms established by Constitutional Law.

Section II. – *The Civil Service*

Article 97

In accordance with European Union law, Government agencies shall ensure that their budgets are balanced and that public debt be sustainable.

Public offices shall be organised under the law and so as to ensure smooth and impartial operation.

Civil service rules shall establish the jurisdiction, duties and responsibilities of civil servants.

Access to the civil service shall be through competitive examinations, except in the cases established by law.

Article 98

Civil servants shall be exclusively at the service of the Nation.

If they are Members of Parliament, they may not be promoted, except through seniority.

The law may set limitations on the right to become members of political parties in the case of magistrates, serving military staff, law enforcement officers, and diplomatic and consular representatives abroad.

Section III. – *Auxiliary Bodies*

Article 99

The National Council for Economics and Labour shall be composed, as set out by law, of experts and representatives of the economic categories, in such a proportion so as to take account of their numerical and qualitative importance.

It shall serve as a consultative body for Parliament and the Government on such matters and functions as may be vested into it by the law.

It may initiate legislation and contribute to drafting economic and social legislation according to the principles and within the limitations set by law.

Article 100

The Council of State shall be a consultative body in administrative law and the guarantor of administrative justice.

A Court of Auditors shall exercise preventive control over the legitimacy of Government measures, and also ex-post auditing on the implementation of the State Budget. It may participate, in such cases and ways as may be established by the law, in auditing the financial management of entities receiving regular budgetary support from the State. It shall report to Parliament on the outcome of its audits.

The law shall ensure that the two bodies above and the members thereof shall be independent of the Government.

TITLE IV
THE JUDICIARY

SECTION I. – *Organisation of the Justice System*

Article 101

Justice shall be administered in the name of the people.

Judges shall be subject only to the law.

Article 102

Judicial proceedings shall be exercised by ordinary magistrates empowered and regulated by the provisions concerning the Judiciary.

Extraordinary or special judges may not be established. Only specialised sections for specific matters within the ordinary judicial bodies may be established, and these sections may include the participation of qualified citizens who are not members of the Judiciary.

The law shall regulate the cases and forms of direct participation of the people in the administration of justice.

Article 103

The Council of State and the other administrative justice bodies shall have jurisdiction over the protection of legitimate interests before public agencies and, in particular matters laid out by the law, also of subjective rights.

The Court of Auditors shall have jurisdiction in matters of public accounts and in other matters laid out by the law.

Military tribunals in times of war shall have the jurisdiction established by the law. In times of peace they shall have jurisdiction only over military offences committed by members of the armed forces.

Article 104

The Judiciary shall be autonomous and independent of all other powers.

The High Council for the Judiciary shall be presided over by the President of the Republic.

The first president and the general prosecutor of the Court of Cassation shall be ex officio members thereof.

Two thirds of its members shall be elected by all ordinary judges belonging to the various categories, and one third shall be elected by Parliament in joint session from among university professors of law and lawyers with fifteen years of practice.

The Council shall elect a vice-president from among the members designated by Parliament.

Elected members of the Council shall remain in office for four years and may not be immediately re-elected.

They may not, while in office, be registered in professional rolls, nor serve in Parliament or on a Regional Council.

Article 105

The High Council for the Judiciary, in accordance with the regulations of the Judiciary, shall have jurisdiction on recruitment, posting and transfer, promotion and disciplinary measures of member of the Judiciary.

Article 106

Judges shall be recruited through competitive examinations.

The law regulating the Judiciary may envisage the appointment, also by election, of honorary judges for all the functions performed by individual judges.

Following a proposal by the High Council for the Judiciary, university professors of law and lawyers with fifteen years of practice and registered in the special professional rolls for the higher courts may be appointed Cassation councillors for their outstanding merits.

Article 107

Judges may not be removed from office; they may not be dismissed or suspended from office or assigned to other courts or functions unless by a decision of the High Council for the Judiciary, taken either for the reasons and in compliance with the defence rights established by the law regulating the Judiciary or with the consent of the judges themselves.

The Minister of Justice shall have the power to originate disciplinary action.

Judges shall be distinguished only by their different functions.

The State prosecutor shall enjoy the safeguards envisaged by the law regulating the Judiciary.

Article 108

The law regulating the Judiciary and its categories shall be an ordinary law.

The law shall ensure the independence of special court judges and prosecutors, and of any outside persons participating in the administration of justice.

Article 109

Criminal police shall be at the service of the Judiciary.

Article 110

Without prejudice to the authority of the High Council for the Judiciary, the Minister of Justice shall have responsibility for the organisation and implementation of services relating to the administration of justice.

Section II. – *Rules on Jurisdiction*

Article 111

Jurisdiction shall be implemented through due process regulated by law.

All court trials shall be conducted with adversary proceedings and parties shall be entitled to equal conditions before a third-party and impartial judge. The law shall provide for a reasonable duration of trials.

In criminal law trials, the law shall establish that the accused be promptly and confidentially informed of the nature and reasons of the charges and be given adequate time and conditions to prepare a defence. A defendant shall have the right to cross-examine witnesses for the prosecution, or to have them cross-examined before a judge; examine witnesses for the defence in the same conditions as the prosecutor; and the right to produce any evidence for the defence. The defendant shall be entitled to the assistance of an interpreter in the case such defendant cannot speak or understand the language in which court proceedings are conducted.

The formation of evidence in criminal law trials shall be based on an adversarial process. The guilt of the defendant may not be established on the basis of statements by persons who have willingly refused cross-examination by the defendant or the defendant's counsel.

The law shall regulate the cases in which the formation of evidence may not occur in an adversarial process, with the consent of the defendant or owing to verified objective impossibility or proven illicit conduct.

All judicial decisions shall include a statement of reasons.

Appeals to the Court of Cassation in cases of violations of the law shall always be allowed against sentences and against measures affecting personal freedom pronounced by ordinary and special courts. This rule can only be waived in cases of sentences by military tribunals in time of war.

Appeals to the Court of Cassation against decisions of the Council of State and the Court of Accounts are permitted only for reasons of jurisdiction.

Article 112

The public prosecutor shall have the obligation to institute criminal proceedings.

Article 113

Judicial protection of legitimate interests and rights against acts of the civil service before bodies of ordinary or administrative justice shall always be permitted.

Such judicial protection may not be excluded or limited to particular kinds of appeal or to particular categories of acts.

The law shall determine which judicial bodies shall be empowered to annul acts of the civil service in the cases and with the consequences provided for by the law itself.

TITLE V

REGIONS, PROVINCES, MUNICIPALITIES

Article 114

The Republic shall be composed of municipalities, provinces, metropolitan cities, regions and the State.

Municipalities, provinces, metropolitan cities and regions shall be autonomous entities having their own statutes, powers and functions in accordance with the principles laid down in the Constitution.

Rome shall be the capital of the Republic. Its status shall be regulated by State Law.

Article 115

[Repealed]

Article 116

Friuli-Venezia Giulia, Sardinia, Sicily, Trentino-Alto Adige/Südtirol and Valle d'Aosta/Vallée d'Aoste shall have special forms and conditions of autonomy pursuant to the special statutes adopted by constitutional law.

The Trentino-Alto Adige/Südtirol Region shall be composed of the autonomous provinces of Trento and Bolzano.

Additional special forms and conditions of autonomy, related to the areas specified in Article 117, paragraph three and paragraph two, letter l) – limited to the organisational requirements of the Justice of the Peace – and letters n) and s) below, may be attributed to Regions by State Law, upon the initiative of the Region concerned, after consultation with the local authorities and in compliance with the principles under Article 119 below. Such State law shall have to be passed by an absolute majority of members in both Houses of Parliament and on the basis of an agreement between the State and the Region concerned.

Article 117

Legislative powers shall be vested in the State and the Regions in compliance with the Constitution and the constraints deriving from EU legislation and international obligations.

The State shall have exclusive legislative powers in the following fields:

a) foreign policy and international relations of the State; relations between the State and the European Union; right of asylum and legal status of non-EU citizens;

b) immigration;

c) relations between the Republic and religious denominations;

d) defence and armed forces; State security; armaments, ammunition and explosives;

e) currency, financial markets and protection of savings; protection of competition; foreign exchange system; state taxation and accounting systems; harmonisation of public accounts; equalisation of financial resources;

f) state bodies and relevant electoral laws; state referendums; elections to the European Parliament;

g) legal and administrative organisation of the State and national governmental agencies;

h) public order and security, with the exception of local administrative police;

i) citizenship, vital records and registry offices;

l) jurisdiction and procedural rules; civil and criminal law; administrative justice;

m) determination of the minimum levels of benefits relating to civil and social entitlements to be ensured throughout the national territory;

n) general provisions on education;

o) social security;

p) electoral legislation, governing bodies and fundamental functions of municipalities, provinces and metropolitan cities;

q) customs, protection of national borders and international preventive healthcare;

r) weights and measures; standard time; statistical and computerised co-ordination of data in state, regional and local administrations; products of the intellect;

s) protection of the environment, the ecosystem and cultural heritage.

Concurrent legislative authority shall apply to the following fields:

international and EU relations of the Regions; foreign trade; job protection and safety; education, subject to the autonomy of educational institutions and with the exception of vocational education and training; professions; scientific and technological research and innovation in support of productive sectors; health protection; nutrition; sports; disaster relief; land-use planning; civil ports and airports; large transport and navigation networks;

regulation of communications; national production, transport and distribution of energy; complementary and supplementary social security; co-ordination of public finance and taxation; enhancement of cultural and environmental assets, including the promotion and organisation of cultural activities; savings banks, rural banks, regional credit institutions; regional land and agricultural credit institutions. In the sectors of concurrent legislation, legislative powers shall be vested in the Regions, except for the determination of fundamental principles, which shall be established by State legislation.

Regions shall have legislative powers in all fields that are not expressly attributed to the State.

The Regions and autonomous provinces of Trento and Bolzano shall take part in the preparatory decision-making process of EU legislative acts in the areas that fall within their responsibilities. They shall also be responsible for the implementation of international agreements and EU measures, subject to the procedural rules set out in State legislation regulating the authority of the State to take over in case of failure to act by Regions or autonomous provinces.

The State shall have regulatory powers in its areas of exclusive legislation, subject to any delegations of such powers to the Regions. Regulatory powers shall be vested in the Regions in all other subject matters. Municipalities, provinces and metropolitan cities shall have regulatory powers as to the organisation and implementation of the functions attributed to them.

Regional laws shall remove any hindrances to the full equality of men and women in social, cultural and economic life and promote equal access to elected offices for men and women.

An agreement between a Region and other Regions aiming to improve the performance of regional functions and also envisaging the establishment of joint bodies shall be ratified by regional law.

In the areas falling within its responsibilities, a Region may enter into agreements with foreign States and local authorities of other States in the cases and according to the forms laid down by State law.

Article 118

Administrative functions shall be vested into municipalities, unless they are attributed to provinces, metropolitan cities and regions or the State, pursuant to the principles of subsidiarity, differentiation and proportionality, in order to ensure uniform implementation.

Municipalities, provinces and metropolitan cities shall have own administrative functions in addition to any functions assigned to them by State or regional legislation, according to their respective competences.

State legislation shall provide for co-ordinated action between the State and the Regions in the fields under Article 117, paragraph two, letters b) and h) above and also provide for agreements and co-ordinated action in the field of the preservation of cultural heritage.

The State, regions, metropolitan cities, provinces and municipalities shall promote the autonomous initiatives of citizens, both as individuals and as members of associations, relating to activities of general interest, on the basis of the principle of subsidiarity.

Article 119

Municipalities, provinces, metropolitan cities and regions shall have revenue and spending autonomy, subject to the obligation to balance their budgets, and shall contribute to ensuring compliance with the economic and financial constraints imposed under European Union legislation.

Municipalities, provinces, metropolitan cities and regions shall have independent financial resources. They may set and levy taxes and collect revenues of their own, in compliance with the Constitution and according to the principles of co-ordination of public finance and the tax system. They shall be entitled to a share of the national revenue originating from their respective territories.

State legislation shall provide for an equalisation fund – to be used with no allocation constraints – for the territories having lower per-capita tax-raising capacity.

Revenues raised from the sources mentioned above shall enable municipalities, provinces, metropolitan cities and regions to fully fund the public functions attributed to them.

The State shall allocate supplementary resources and adopt special measures in favour of specific municipalities, provinces, metropolitan cities and regions to promote economic development along with social cohesion and solidarity, to eliminate economic and social imbalances, to foster the exercise of the rights of the person or to achieve goals other than those pursued in the ordinary implementation of their functions.

Municipalities, provinces, metropolitan cities and regions shall have their own assets, which are allocated to them pursuant to general principles under State law. They may have recourse to borrowing only as a means of funding investment, in conjunction with the definition of amortisation plans and subject to the condition that the comprehensive budget of all local authorities in the region be balanced. State collateral on borrowings by such authorities shall not be admissible.

Article 120

A Region may not levy import or export or transit duties between Regions, nor adopt measures that in any way obstruct freedom of movement of persons or goods between Regions. A Region may not limit the right of citizens to work in any part whatsoever of the national territory.

The Government can subsume the authority of a Region, metropolitan city, province or municipality if it fails to comply with international rules and treaties or EU legislation, or in case of grave danger for public safety and security, or whenever such action is necessary in order to preserve legal or economic unity and in particular to ensure the minimum level of benefits relating to civil and social entitlements, regardless of the geographic borders of a local authority. The law shall lay down the procedures to ensure that subsidiary powers are exercised in compliance with the principles of subsidiarity and loyal co-operation.

Article 121

The bodies of the Region are: the Regional Council, the Regional Government and its President.

The Regional Council shall exercise the legislative powers attributed to the Region and the other functions conferred by the Constitution and the laws. It may submit bills to Parliament.

The Regional Government shall be the executive body of the Region.

The President of the Government shall represent the Region, set and be accountable for regional policies, promulgate regional laws and regulations, direct the administrative functions delegated to the Region by the State in compliance with the instructions of the Government of the Republic.

Article 122

The regional electoral system and the causes for disqualification and incompatibility of the President, the other members of the Regional Government and the Regional councillors shall be established by regional law in accordance with the fundamental principles established by a law of the Republic, which shall also establish the terms of elected offices.

No-one may belong at the same time to a Regional Council or a Regional Government and either House of Parliament, another Regional Council, or the European Parliament.

The Council shall elect a President and a Bureau from amongst its members.

Regional councillors may not be held accountable for the opinions expressed and votes cast in the exercise of their functions.

The President of a Regional Government shall be elected by universal and direct suffrage, unless the regional statute provides otherwise. The elected President shall appoint and dismiss members of the regional Government.

Article 123

Each Region shall have a statute which, in compliance with the Constitution, shall lay down the form of government and basic principles for the organisation of the Region and the conduct of its business. The statute shall regulate the right to initiate legislation and promote referendums on regional laws and administrative measures and the publication of laws and regional regulations.

Regional statutes shall be adopted and amended by a Regional Council by law approved by an absolute majority of its members, in two subsequent decisions at an interval of no less than two months. Such law shall not require the approval of the Government Commissioner. The Government of the Republic may challenge the constitutional legitimacy of a regional statute before the Constitutional Court within thirty days of its publication.

Such statute shall be submitted to referendum if one-fiftieth of the electors of the Region or one-fifth of the members of the Regional Council so request within three months of its publication. A statute that is submitted to referendum may not be promulgated unless approved by a majority of valid votes.

In each Region, statutes shall regulate the activity of a Council of local authorities, a consultative body on relations between the Regions and local authorities.

Article 124

[Repealed]

Article 125

First-tier administrative courts shall be established in the Regions, in accordance with the rules established by law of the Republic. Sections of such courts may be established in places other than the regional capital.

Article 126

A Regional Council may be dissolved and a President of the Government may be removed by reasoned decree of the President of the Republic in case of acts in contrast with the Constitution or grave violations of the law. Dissolution or removal may also be decided for reasons of national security. Such a decree shall be adopted after consultation with a committee of deputies and senators for regional affairs which shall be established in the manner established by a law of the Republic.

A Regional Council may adopt a reasoned motion of no confidence against the President of the Government that shall be undersigned by at least one-fifth of its members and adopted by roll call vote with an absolute majority of members. The motion may not be debated before three days have elapsed since its introduction.

The adoption of a no confidence motion against a President of a Regional Government elected by universal and direct suffrage, and the removal, permanent inability, death or voluntary resignation of the President of the Regional Government shall entail the resignation of the Government and the dissolution of the Council. The same effect shall be produced by the simultaneous resignation of the majority of the Council members.

Article 127

The central Government may challenge the constitutional compliance of a regional law before the Constitutional Court within sixty days of its publication, if it deems that such law exceeds the jurisdiction of the Region.

A Region may challenge the constitutional compliance of a law or measure having the force of law adopted by the State or by another Region before the Constitutional Court within sixty days of its publication, if it deems that such law or measure infringes upon its competence.

Article 128

[Repealed]

Article 129

[Repealed]

Article 130

[Repealed]

Article 131

The following Regions shall be established:

Piedmont;
Valle d'Aosta;
Lombardy;
Trentino-Alto Adige;
Veneto;
Friuli-Venezia Giulia;
Liguria;
Emilia-Romagna;
Tuscany;
Umbria;
Marche;
Latium;
Abruzzi;
Molise;
Campania;
Apulia;
Basilicata;
Calabria;
Sicily;
Sardinia.

Article 132

Following consultation with the regional Councils, a Constitutional amendment law merging existing Regions or creating new Regions with a minimum of one million inhabitants may be agreed, if such request has been made by a number of municipal Councils representing no less than one third of the population involved and has been approved by referendum by a majority of such population.

A province or municipality requesting to be detached from a region and incorporated into another may be allowed to do so, following a successful referendum in the provinces and municipalities concerned, after consultation with regional Councils and passage of a State law.

Article 133

Changes in provincial borders and the establishment of a new province within a region shall be regulated by the laws of the Republic, upon the initiative of a municipality and after consultation with the region.

The Region, after consultation with the population involved, may adopt legislation to establish new municipalities within its own borders and modify their districts and names.

TITLE VI

CONSTITUTIONAL SAFEGUARDS

SECTION I. – *The Constitutional Court*

Article 134

The Constitutional Court shall pass judgement on:

controversies on the constitutional legitimacy of laws and measures having force of law issued by the State and Regions;

conflicts of authority between central institutions, between State and Regions, and between Regions;

charges brought against the President of the Republic, according to the provisions of the Constitution.

Article 135

The Constitutional Court shall be composed of fifteen judges, a third nominated by the President of the Republic, a third by Parliament in joint sitting and a third by the ordinary and administrative supreme Courts.

The judges of the Constitutional Courts shall be chosen from among judges, including those retired, of higher ordinary and administrative Courts, university professors of law and lawyers with at least twenty years practice.

Judges of the Constitutional Court shall be appointed for nine years, beginning in each case from the day of their oath, and may not be re-appointed.

At the expiry of his or her term, a constitutional judge shall leave office and the exercise of its functions.

The Court shall elect from among its members, in accordance with the rules established by law, a President, who shall remain in office for three years and may be re-elected, in accordance with the term for constitutional judges.

The office of constitutional judge shall be incompatible with membership of Parliament, of a Regional Council, the practice of the legal profession, and any office pursuant to the law.

In impeachment proceedings against the President of the Republic the ordinary judges of the Court shall be supplemented with sixteen members chosen by lot from among a list of citizens qualified to be elected to the Senate, which Parliament shall draw every nine years through an election using the same procedures as the appointment of ordinary judges.

Article 136

A law or any other measure declared by the Court not to be compliant with the Constitution shall cease to have effect on the day following the publication of the decision.

A Court decision shall be published and transmitted to Parliament and the Regional Councils concerned, so that, if they deem it necessary, they may act in conformity with the Constitution.

Article 137

A constitutional law shall establish the conditions, forms, terms for proposing judgements on constitutional compliance, and the safeguards on the independence of constitutional judges.

An ordinary law shall establish any other provisions necessary for the establishment and functioning of the Court.

A decision of the Constitutional Court may not be appealed against.

Section II. – *Amendments to the Constitution. Constitutional Laws*

Article 138

A law amending the Constitution or any other constitutional law shall be adopted by each House after two successive debates at intervals of no less than three months and by an absolute majority of the members of each House in the second vote.

A law so adopted may be submitted to referendum if, within three months of its publication, such request is made by one-fifth of the members of a House of Parliament or five hundred thousand voters or five Regional Councils. A law submitted to referendum may not be promulgated unless approved by a majority of valid votes.

A referendum shall not be held if a law was approved in the second vote in both Houses by a majority of two-thirds of the members.

Article 139

The status of Republic may not be subject to constitutional amendment.

TRANSITIONAL AND FINAL PROVISIONS

I

Following entry into force of the Constitution, the provisional Head of State shall exercise the functions of President of the Republic and assume that title.

II

If, on the date of the election of the President of the Republic, not all Regional Councils have been established, only members of the two Houses shall participate in the election.

III

By decree of the President of the Republic, the first Senate of the Republic shall be formed by all deputies to the Constituent Assembly who possess prerequisites to be senators and who:

were Presidents of the Council of Ministers or of legislative Assemblies;

were members of the dissolved Senate;

were elected at least three times including to the Constituent Assembly;

were disqualified at the sitting of the Chamber of deputies of 9 November 1926;

were imprisoned for no less than five years following a sentence of the special Fascist tribunal for the defence of the State.

Members of the dissolved Senate who were also members of the Consulta Nazionale shall be appointed Senators by decree of the President of the Republic.

The right to be appointed senator may be renounced before signing the decree of appointment. Acceptance of candidacy in political elections shall constitute renunciation of the right to be appointed senator.

IV

For the first election of the Senate, Molise shall be considered a Region in itself, having the due number of Senators on the basis of its population.

V

The provisions of Article 80 of the Constitution on the question of international treaties which involve budget expenditures or changes in the law shall become effective as from the date of convocation of Parliament.

VI

Within five years after the Constitution has come into effect, the special courts still in existence shall be revised, with the exception of the Council of State, the Court of Auditors and the military courts.

Within a year of the same date, a law shall provide for the re-organisation of the Supreme Military Tribunal according to Article 111.

VII

Until such time as the new law on the Judiciary under this Constitution has been issued, the provisions in force shall continue to be observed.

Until such time as the Constitutional Court begins its functions, decision on controversies as per Article 134 shall be conducted in the forms and within the limits of the provisions already in existence before the implementation of the Constitution.

VIII

Elections of the Regional Councils and the elected bodies of provincial administration shall be called within one year of the implementation of the Constitution.

The laws of the Republic shall regulate for every branch of public administration the passage of the state functions attributed to the Regions. Until such time as the re-organisation and re-distribution of the administrative functions among the local bodies has been accomplished, the provinces and municipalities shall retain those functions they presently exercise and others which the Regions may delegate to them.

The laws of the Republic shall regulate the transfer to the Regions of State officials and employees, including from central administrations, which shall be necessary under the new provisions. In setting up their offices, Regions shall, except in cases of necessity, draw their personnel from among the employees of local State agencies.

IX

Within three years of implementation of the Constitution, the Republic shall adjust its laws to the needs of local government and the legislative authority attributed to Regions.

X

The general provisions of Title V of the Second Part of this Constitution shall temporarily apply to the Region of Friuli-Venezia Giulia, as per Article 116, without prejudice to the protection of linguistic minorities in accordance with Article 6.

XI

Up to five years following implementation of the Constitution, other Regions may be established by constitutional law, thus amending the list under Article 131 above, also in default of the conditions under the first paragraph of Article 132 above, without prejudice, however, to the obligation to consult with the population concerned.

XII

It shall be forbidden to reorganise, under any form whatsoever, the dissolved Fascist party.

Notwithstanding Article 48 above, the law has established, for no more than five years following the entry into force of the Constitution, temporary limitations to the right to vote and eligibility of leaders of the Fascist regime.

XIII[1]

The members and descendants of the House of Savoy shall not be voters and may not hold public office or elected offices.

Access and sojourn in the national territory shall be forbidden to the former kings of the House of Savoy, their spouses and their male descendants. The assets, existing on national territory, of the former kings of the House of Savoy, their spouses and their male descendants shall be transferred to the State. Transfers and the establishment of royal rights on said properties after 2 June 1946 shall be null and void.

XIV

Titles of nobility shall not be recognised.

The place-names included in those existing before 28 October 1922 shall serve as part of the name.

The Order of Saint Mauritius shall be preserved as a hospital corporation and shall function in the ways established by law.

The law shall regulate the suppression of the Heraldry Council.

XV

Following entry into force of the Constitution, the legislative decree of the Lieutenant of the Kingdom No. 151 of 25 June 1944 on the provisional organisation

[1] The single article of Constitutional Amendment Law 23 October 2002, no. 1 on the Expiry of the Thirteenth Transitional and Final Provision of the Constitution (published in *Gazzetta Ufficiale* no. 252 of 26 October 2002) establishes that "the first and second paragraphs of the 13th transitional and final provision of the Constitution shall cease to have effect following entry into force of this Constitutional Amendment Law."

of the State shall become law.

XVI

Within a year of entry into force of the Constitution, the revision and co-ordination of previous constitutional laws which have not at that moment been explicitly or implicitly repealed shall begin.

XVII

The Constituent Assembly shall be called by its President to decide, before 31 January 1948, on the law for the election of the Senate of the Republic, the special regional statues and the law governing the press.

Until the day of the election of a new Parliament, the Constituent Assembly may be convened, when it is necessary to decide on matters attributed to its jurisdiction by Article 2, paragraphs one and two, and Article 3, paragraphs one and two, of legislative decree No. 98 of 16 March 1946.

In this period, standing committees shall maintain their functions. Legislative committees may submit to the Government their comments and proposed amendments on bills introduced before them.

Deputies may put questions to the Government requesting a written answer.

In accordance with the second paragraph above, the Constituent Assembly shall be convened by its President following a reasoned request of the Government or at least two hundred deputies.

XVIII

This Constitution shall be promulgated by the provisional Head of State within five days of its approval by the Constituent Assembly and shall come into force on 1st January 1948.

The text of the Constitution shall be deposited in the Town Hall of every municipality of the Republic and be kept on display there, for the whole of 1948, so as to allow every citizen to know of it.

The Constitution, bearing the seal of the State, shall be included in the Official Record of the laws and decrees of the Republic.

The Constitution must be faithfully observed as the fundamental law of the Republic by all citizens and bodies of the State.

Given in Rome on this 27th Day of December 1947

ENRICO DE NICOLA

COUNTERSIGNED

The President of the Constituent Assembly	*The President of the Council of Ministers*
UMBERTO TERRACINI	ALCIDE DE GASPERI

IN WITNESS WHEREOF

The Keeper of the Seal

GIUSEPPE GRASSI

Printed by Libri Plureos GmbH in Hamburg,
Germany